6/8/05   Scholastic $22.00

LSTA Grant
Weed + Feed 2005

Way of the
Warrior

VIKINGS
Raiders and Explorers

Aileen Weintraub

HIGH
interest
books

Children's Press®
A Division of Scholastic Inc.
New York / Toronto / London / Auckland / Sydney
Mexico City / New Delhi / Hong Kong
Danbury, Connecticut

Book Design: Michael DeLisio and Elana Davidian
Contributing Editor: Matthew Pitt
Photo Credits: Cover, p. 5 © Hulton/Archive/Getty Images; pp. 6, 13, 28 ©
Bettmann/Corbis; p. 8 © maps.com/Corbis; pp. 10, 38 © Ted Spiegel/Corbis; pp. 15,
25, 31 © North Wind Picture Archives; p. 18 © Private Collection/Bridgeman Art
Library; p. 21 © Viking Ship Museum, Oslo, Norway/Bridgeman Art Library; p. 22
© Nationalmuseet, Copenhagen, Denmark/Bridgeman Art Library; p. 34 © Private
Collection/The Stapleton Collection/Bridgeman Art Library; p. 27 © Jason Lindsey;
p. 40 © Richard T. Nowitz/Corbis

Library of Congress Cataloging-in-Publication Data

Weintraub, Aileen, 1973–
    Vikings : raiders and explorers / Aileen Weintraub.
    p. cm. — (Way of the warrior)
    Includes index.
    ISBN 0-516-25118-X (lib. bdg.) — ISBN 0-516-25087-6 (pbk.)
    1. Vikings. I. Title. II. Series.

    DL65.W38 2005
    948'.022—dc22

                                                        2004003276

1 2 3 4 5 6 7 8 9 10 R 14 13 12 11 10 09 08 07 06 05

Contents

INTRODUCTION

The men quietly docked their boats. They had just spent the last few days sailing on the high seas. Now they had reached the shores of Lindisfarne, an island off England's eastern coastline. It was summer 793. A fearsome image of a dragon's head was carved into the front of each of their ships.

Minutes later, these men burst into a monastery, drawing their swords and axes. The people who lived and worked inside the monastery were terrified. The fierce and brutal warriors killed those who got in their way. Within minutes, blood covered the church floor. The warriors stole the church's treasures. They even stripped objects of art off the walls. Then, as quickly as they came, they disappeared.

A monk who survived the raid later described the scene: "Attackers spread in all directions like horrible wolves, wrecking, robbing, shattering, and killing not only animals but also priests, monks, and nuns."

This painting shows Vikings returning from their raid on Lindisfarne.

Exactly who were these attackers that would do such things? For a long time, there was no definite answer. At first, they were known simply as Northmen. Later, the attackers would be called Vikings. This was one of the Vikings' first major raids, but it would hardly be their last. For the next three hundred years, their reign of terror would continue.

CHAPTER ONE

Strangers From the North

The Vikings left behind very few written records. Many of the records they did leave behind are unreliable and tell us very little about their lives. Yet the image of a fierce Viking warrior doing battle with axe and spear lives in history to this day. How have historians learned about the travels and violent conquests of these ancient warriors?

For centuries, historians relied on a document called *The Anglo-Saxon Chronicle*. The *Chronicle* was started by English king

The Vikings were imposing warriors whose fierce attacks on eastern and western Europe changed the course of history.

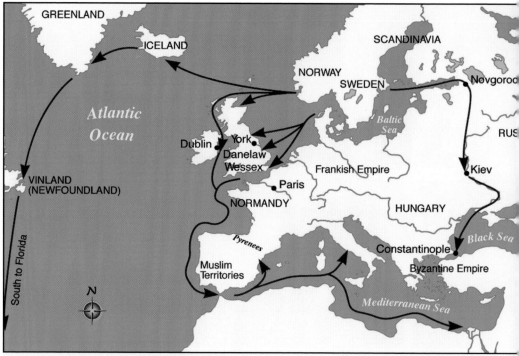

As master navigators, the Vikings were able to travel to many parts of the world. This map shows numerous Viking exploration routes throughout Europe and toward the New World of the Americas.

Alfred the Great in 890. It contains information about the Vikings' activities in Europe and their encounters with people living there. For instance, the *Chronicle* reported that in 789 an Englishman warmly greeted the newcomers who had arrived near his coastal home. The newcomers were Vikings. They killed the man immediately.

The Way of the Viking

In the eighth century, churches and monasteries were considered safe from attack. The monks, priests, and nuns who lived in them carried no weapons. They had no way of defending themselves against attackers. Armies refused to attack churches, because they believed these were holy places. Vikings, however, had no loyalty to the Christian church. They simply knew that churches and monasteries held gold and silver. The Vikings raided these places for all the treasure they could find.

Vikings also took people as their slaves. They often captured women and children, forcing them to work against their will. Some rowed the Vikings' boats. Others helped the Vikings set up new villages. Some slaves were allowed to farm land. If these farms produced healthy crops, the slaves could buy their freedom.

FIGHTING WORDS

Vikings originally came from an area called Scandinavia. These nations, in northern Europe, are known today as Denmark, Sweden, and Norway.

Savage Warriors?

The Anglo-Saxon Chronicle describes the Vikings mostly as savage warriors. In recent years, though, historians have discovered that Vikings did more than just raid and fight. They were skilled traders, farmers, fishermen, and craftsmen. They made many of their tools from iron found in the bogs of Northern Europe. They were able to shape this iron into sickles, picks, and other tools.

The Vikings have also been recognized as talented explorers. Sailing in their giant boats, they were able to reach regions as far away as North Africa. They traded their goods with Arab merchants, bringing back glass and spices. In other places, Vikings exchanged fur and slaves for precious metals. They worked these metals into beautiful rings, bracelets, and necklaces.

Erik's Trek and Trick

Erik the Red was considered one of the greatest Viking leaders and explorers. As a young boy, Erik's father killed a man during an argument in Norway. Erik and his family were cast out of their homeland. They were forced to move to Iceland.

After a few years of living in Iceland, Erik the Red got into a heated fight. It is believed he killed two men during the fight. A Viking elder found him guilty of the crime and, like his father, Erik was banished from his home.

In this photo, Viking coins lie on a page of *The Anglo-Saxon Chronicle*. This part of the *Chronicle* describes the Vikings living through a winter in England for the first time.

11

Rounding up a group of friends, Erik sailed west of Iceland. Erik's crew soon discovered new land. Most of it was covered with glaciers. The dirt was frozen. However, Erik found land near the sea that he was able to farm.

Erik the Red's punishment ended three years later. He returned to Iceland, hoping to convince people to join him in the new lands he had discovered. He called his lands Greenland, believing this name would convince others to join him. Erik's trick worked. Many Vikings followed Erik to Greenland. Thanks to Erik the Red's leadership, Greenland's population soared for many years.

Leif the Lucky

Born around 980, Leif Erikson was Erik the Red's son. Like many Viking boys, Leif spent much of his childhood apart from his family. From an early age, boys were trained to become strong, fierce warriors.

This painting shows Leif Erikson (standing) sailing off the coast of North America. He later named this land Vinland.

At the age of eight, Leif began studying with a man named Thyrker. Thyrker was a German who Erik the Red had captured during a raid. Thyrker taught Leif how to read and write. He also taught Leif how to trade goods and speak in different languages. Most of all, he taught Leif how to be a fearless warrior.

After Leif's training, he and his father set sail on many voyages. During a trip home to Greenland, Leif saved a crew whose ship had been in a wreck. Leif was given the ship's cargo as a reward. For this, he became known as Leif the Lucky.

Leif's most famous journey took him to the North American continent. He was the

first European to land there—nearly five hundred years before Christopher Columbus! Experts have different opinions about why Leif made this trip. Some claim that his ship was simply blown off course. Others suggest that Leif heard about North America from a fellow Viking sailor. This sailor had once seen the new continent when his ship went off course. Leif's curiosity may have led him to repeat his friend's voyage.

Whatever the case, Leif probably reached North America around the year 1000. He found a coast filled with meadows, trees, and wild grapes. Leif's luck had struck again! He named this new land Vinland. Historians believe that Leif's crew landed on the northern tip of what is now called Newfoundland, an island off the coast of Canada.

Legends and Myths

The Viking religion was based on the idea that there were many gods. These gods played an

Explorer Thorfinn and his wife, Gudrid, led an expedition from Greenland to Vinland in about 1004. Their son, Snorri, born in 1005, is believed to be the first European born on the mainland of North America. This painting shows them at their landing in Vinland.

important role in Viking life. Vikings often asked gods to help them through their difficult times and travels. Vikings told many stories about their powerful gods.

Odin—the god of war, wisdom, justice, and poetry—was the most powerful god in the Viking religion. He is often portrayed as having only one eye. Viking legends tell us that Odin gave up his other eye in exchange for wisdom. He also rode a horse that had eight legs, so it would never get tired.

Odin's eldest son, Thor the Thunderer, protected the universe. Thor was the god of sailors, farmers, and the sky. Able to control storms, Thor could even send powerful thunderbolts crashing to Earth. Thor was famous for his hammer, *Mjoollinor*, which means "the destroyer" in the Old Norse language. When Thor threw this weapon at

THE VALKYRIES

Odin's nine daughters were called the Valkyries. They flew over battlefields on winged horses and decided which Vikings would live or die.

Valkyries saved only the bravest warriors. These lucky warriors would be carried to Odin's banquet hall, called Valhalla. There, the warriors' battle wounds would suddenly vanish. Then they would spend eternity feasting in Valhalla and fighting by Odin's side.

an enemy, it would always magically return to his hand.

Many Vikings wore a silver hammer around their necks to honor Thor. Thor continues to be honored today in our calendars. This god's name is the basis of the word Thursday (Thor's day).

Giant Problems

Viking sagas tell tales of fierce battles between the gods and enormous giants. Vikings believed the world would end with a fierce battle between the gods and these giants. This battle was called *Ragnarök*. Fire would break out and the world would be torn apart. According to the myth, a great wolf would swallow the sun. Only two humans, who were in hiding, would survive the terrible event. They would have to start a new world. No wonder Vikings felt they had to keep their combat skills sharp!

CHAPTER TWO

Waging War

Shipshape

Vikings were skilled sailors and boatbuilders. The impressive vessels they used in exploration and raiding were called long ships. Long ships were very light and fast and could hold a crew of up to one hundred men.

Long ships were made of long planks of overlapping timber. The timber was raised high in both the prow and stern (front and back) of the boats. This style of building made Viking voyages over rough waters go more smoothly. Crossbeams were put in place for a deck and rowing benches. The Vikings put pine tar on the wood to make their long ships waterproof.

The Vikings were master shipbuilders. The ships' bottoms were built so that the ships rode high in the water, skimming the surface for speed.

The *drakar* was a type of long ship that
Vikings used to sail across the ocean. *Drakars*
often featured a dragon's head carved into
their prows. This fearsome decoration was a
signal to their victims that they had come to
fight. On their way to a raid, Vikings raised a
square sail. This sail would catch high winds,
pushing the Vikings across the sea. Once they
got near their target, they lowered the sail and
rowed the *drakar* with oars. Oars allowed
Vikings to row through narrow passageways
along a coastline. *Drakars* could be rowed
right up to the beach. Once they landed, the
crews could immediately launch their attacks.

Over time, Vikings developed other types
of ships. One of these was the *knarr*. The
knarr was higher and wider than a long ship
and had fewer oars. It was able to hold
massive amounts of cargo. Vikings used this
ship when trading over great distances.

Beautifully carved figureheads appeared on the front of many
Viking boats. This figurehead, which looks like a dragon or
serpent, is from a Viking long ship that was found in Norway.
The figurehead dates back to the ninth century.

Axes were not only deadly weapons in the hands of a Viking warrior, but they were often carved with fine decorations. This axe-head is in a museum in Denmark.

On the Battlefield

Vikings were always prepared for battle. They used axes, spears, and swords during combat. A sword's handle was often decorated with precious metals. Viking warriors preferred using double-edged swords. This way, they knew they would wound their enemies no matter which side of the sword struck them.

FIGHTING WORDS

Viking warriors took such pride in their weapons that they often gave them nicknames like "Long and Sharp" and "Leg Biter."

The battle-axe may be the most well-known Viking weapon. Vikings used two types of axes. One was held in the hand and swung at enemies. A lighter axe was thrown with tremendous force. Blows from battle-axes were usually fatal. Vikings were also known for using spears and knives. The most skilled warriors could throw two spears at once. Some Vikings could even catch an enemy's spear in flight and hurl it back!

A Warrior's Wardrobe

Vikings almost always engaged in hand-to-hand combat. During this type of fighting, Vikings used circular shields to protect themselves. Their shields were made of wood and leather and had iron handgrips. They were often painted in bright colors. Around the year 1000, shields were redesigned. Vikings began building their shields in the shape of kites, which gave better protection to warriors' legs. Vikings used helmets made of leather or metal to protect their heads from injury. Metal helmets featured noseguards for extra protection. However, these helmets were not topped with horns, as many people believe.

Raised to Fight

Viking boys often followed in their fathers' footsteps. If their fathers had been trained as warriors, they would receive the same training. They grew up learning the skills required for waging war. They spent more time wrestling than learning arithmetic. Their elders shared many myths about brave war heroes who conquered land and claimed treasure. Young warriors hoped that by serving important leaders, they would be rewarded with their own fame and wealth.

This illustration shows Vikings as they prepare for a raid.

Crimes and Punishment

Vikings usually did not have a formal
government or written laws. Instead, they
held local meetings where they discussed
common interests. At some of these meetings,
Vikings would share secrets about hunting
and fishing with one another. More often,

these meetings were held to settle fights or
disputes between Vikings. This was usually
done with money. If money didn't solve the
problem, the Viking being punished would be
banished. As a last resort, the arguing parties
would duel to the death.

Viking Runes

The Vikings did not use the same alphabet we
use today. The form of lettering used by Vikings
is known as runes. Vikings did not have paper
to write on, so they chiseled the runes into
stone and other objects. Vikings deeply
respected runes, believing them to be a gift
from Odin. They believed that anyone who
could read runes had the power to cure
illnesses and break through chains.

Runes were used for many reasons. Vikings
labeled their personal belongings with them.
They carved runes into their weapons, believing
they would make the weapon more powerful.
After a successful raid, Vikings often carved

This rune stone is located near Stockholm, Sweden. The red
coloring has been added to make the runes easier to see. Many
stones are decorated with pictures of snakes, horses, and ships.

runes into statues in the town. Runes were also carved into memorial stones to honor warriors killed in battle. Almost three thousand of these stones have been found in Scandinavia.

Runes are a valuable source of Viking history. However, they do not give a full picture of events or people, because texts were not very long.

CHAPTER THREE

Terror on the Move

For much of the long, cold winter, Vikings planned which sites they were going to attack. Viking kings approved some of the largest raids. Most raids, however, were thought up by a small band of warriors who were simply greedy for treasure.

Once the summer began, the warriors went into attack mode. Sailing to their raid, they hung dozens of shields over the sides of their long ships. This helped protect both the crew and the ship from enemy arrows. It was also done for show. The Vikings were signaling to their victims that they weren't sailing in for a visit. They were coming to fight.

This painting shows Vikings landing off the coast of France. In 911, France gave the territory now called Normandy to Viking leader Rollo. In exchange, Rollo promised to defend France against other Vikings. Rollo's Vikings were called Normans.

Although Vikings rarely battled on the open seas, they were prepared to do so. If Viking warriors spotted enemy ships closing in, they'd bind their fleet of long ships together with thick rope. Once the enemy drew close enough, the Viking fleet would launch a shower of arrows and spears at their ships.

The best Viking warriors stood at the ship's prow. As the enemy drew closer, these warriors leaped onto the enemy's ships. They weren't trying to sink the enemy vessels. They were trying to capture them! They were also looking for any treasures that had been stored on board.

Fear and Brutality

Most Viking battles, however, took place on land. Once their long ships reached shore, the Vikings went after their surprised victims. Their style of fighting wasn't very organized. That's probably why Vikings preferred sneak attacks. When they fought large battles against well-trained armies, they usually weren't as successful.

Still, the Vikings did use a few fighting strategies. Once they reached the shore, the youngest Vikings often lined up in front.

This painting shows Viking raiders being attacked by natives. It is thought that this occurred on the coast of Canada in about 1002.

Each young Viking overlapped his shield with the shield of the warrior standing beside him. In this way, they formed a solid wall that protected the more experienced Vikings from enemy arrows. Someone would throw a spear over enemy lines to dedicate the battle to Odin. Then, without further warning, a shower of spears rained down on the enemy.

Vikings were also known to get into a formation called the *svinfylking*. Vikings used this formation to overpower their enemies. About thirty Vikings lined up in the shape of a V—the point of the V faced the enemy. All at once, the Vikings charged, trying to break through enemy lines with their great weight and numbers.

Going Berserk

No Vikings fought as wildly as the Berserkers. This group of warriors painted their faces before fights. They sometimes dressed like wild animals and wore animal skins instead of clothes or armor. Some reports of Beserkers say they fought naked. However, all the legends agree that Berserkers *acted* like wild animals. They worked themselves into a state of rage just before a raid began. They'd start to shiver, their teeth would chatter. While in this vicious state, they bit off pieces of their own shields and howled like wolves. During battle, Berserkers were able to ignore pain. They shrugged off the blows from their enemies' weapons.

Their fierceness shocked villagers, often causing them to surrender. While Berserkers were thought of as great fighters, most Vikings didn't trust them. Berserkers were known to get so crazy during a battle that they'd attack their own friends! In 1015, one Viking leader made it a crime to be a Berserker.

FIGHTING WORDS

Some village leaders were so afraid of raids that their leaders paid off the Vikings in advance.

K. WILLIAM Y CONQVEROR

CHAPTER FOUR

End of an Era

Trading Faiths

Vikings raided many people and traded with many cultures. Yet they took more than treasure when they explored a new land. Sometimes, they took on the ideas and beliefs of a new group of people.

In 984, Leif Erikson sailed to Norway. He brought gifts to Norway's ruler, King Olaf. Olaf told Leif that a terrible disease had swept across his land. Many of his people died from the disease. Once the king embraced the Christian faith, the disease ended. Moved by this change in fortune, Leif decided to start following this new faith as well.

In 1066, William, the Duke of Normandy, became king of England. He won the Battle of Hastings against King Harold. One of the main reasons William won was because Harold's army was busy fighting off a Viking invasion in another part of England!

The Vikings were happy to accept the Christian faith. For them, this decision simply meant believing in one more god. It also helped the Vikings make more money. That's because Christians weren't supposed to trade with those who didn't share their faith. Once Vikings accepted this new religion, Christians began to trade freely with them.

Sea Change

The battle for control of England raged for many years. In the ninth century, the Vikings were forced away from western England. However, they took England back in 1016, led by their king, Knut. Their control of the country only lasted a short time though. In 1042, they were driven out.

In 1066, Vikings tried to reconquer England. The Vikings raided coastal villages in the north and captured the town of York. England's King Harold sent most of his army to stop the invaders. A fierce battle was fought in York as the English army destroyed the Viking forces. The Vikings never mounted another significant raid against England. The end of the Viking era was near.

A change in the style of combat also led to the end of the Viking era. It became common for towns to pay soldiers for protection. Villages that were once defenseless now had armies at their command. These trained soldiers were much more prepared for Viking sneak attacks. They rode on horseback and were heavily armed. Viking warriors found they had met their match.

FIGHTING WORDS

Vikings often watched birds, whales, and even bugs to find out which direction they should sail! For instance, they knew that fleas always hopped north, so they used them as a kind of compass.

Fuzzy History

The Vikings remain mysterious to this day. Finding records about their raids and ways of life is very difficult. Vikings didn't record things on paper. Instead, they carved letters into rune stones. Because of this, Vikings left very few written accounts behind. In addition, most of the stones that have been found give only brief accounts of historical events. They do very little to describe Viking customs.

Much of what we know about Vikings comes from Christian records. However, the

reports may not be very accurate. They were often written by Vikings' enemies. Sagas are another way we can learn about Viking history. They give more details than runes. However, many sagas were written hundreds of years after the events they describe. Experts suspect that many of their details have been made up. While they can give us clues about the past, they won't give us the whole story.

Physical Clues

Without many written records, how can we learn more about Viking life? One way is to dig for the answers. To date, archaeologists have uncovered many items used by Vikings. These include beautiful pieces of jewelry, weapons, fabric, and even entire Viking long ships!

Two ships in particular have excited people interested in Viking culture. The ships were unearthed in Norway in 1880 and 1906.

This photo shows workers searching for ancient Viking objects and footpaths in Dublin, Ireland. The Vikings created new towns in Ireland, such as Dublin and Limerick, which became major cities in later years.

They had been purposely buried in pits of waterlogged clay and covered with stones and earth. Archaeologists believe that the bodies of dead Vikings were put on the ships, which were then buried. We do not know who the dead were, but perhaps they belonged to a royal family. Animal remains, cooking tools, beds, and tents were also found on the ships. Archaeologists want to determine if burying the dead in this way was a common practice in Viking culture.

The clay in which the long ships were buried protected them from serious damage. Scientists were able to learn when and where the ships were built by studying the tree rings in the ships' wood.

These discoveries teach us about the sailing and building skills of the Vikings. They let us know how the Vikings lived and how these warriors conquered the seas. By continuing this kind of work, the mysteries and myths of Vikings may slowly be unraveled and solved.

This Viking ship sits in a museum in Oslo, Norway. It was built around 850–900. Called the Oseberg Ship, it is one of the best-preserved Viking long ships ever discovered.

41

New Words

archaeologists (ar-kee-**ol**-o-gists) people who learn about the past by digging up old objects and examining them carefully

banish (**ban**-ish) to send someone away from a place and order the person not to return

chisel (**chiz**-uhl) to chip away at something and form it into a desired shape

chronicle (**kron**-uh-kuhl) a detailed recording of historical events

glaciers (**glay**-shurz) huge sheets of ice found in mountain valleys or polar regions

long ships (**long ships**) long, narrow ships with many oars and a sail, used especially by the Vikings

monasteries (**mon**-uh-ster-eez) groups of buildings where monks live and work

New Words

prow (**prou**) the bow or front part of a boat or ship

raid (**rayd**) a sudden, surprise attack on a place

runes (**roonz**) letters in the written alphabet of Vikings, usually carved onto stones

sagas (**sa**-gas) long stories about Viking heroes and events passed down through generations

sickles (**sik**-uhlz) tools with short handles and curved blades that are used for cutting grain, grass, or weeds

stern (**stern**) the back end of a boat or ship

unravel (uhn-**rav**-uhl) to search for and discover the truth about a complex situation

For Further Reading

Jovinelly, Joann, and Jason Netelkos. *The Crafts and Culture of the Vikings*. New York: Rosen Publishing Group, Inc., 2001.

Lassieur, Allison. *The Vikings*. Farmington Hills, MI: Lucent Books, 2001.

Margeson, Susan M. *Viking*. New York: DK Publishing, Inc., 2000.

Ross, Stewart. *Vikings*. Brookfield, CT: Millbrook Press, 2000.

RESOURCES

Organizations

The Gothenburg Viking Ship Society
Box 11488
S-404 30
Göteborg, Sweden

The Viking Society of Northern Research
University College of London
Gower Street
London, England WCIE 6 BT

Resources

Web Sites

Nova Online—The Vikings
www.pbs.org/wgbh/nova/vikings/
This Web site is a companion to a two-hour
television program on PBS about the Vikings.
It's filled with maps, videos, and great facts
about long ships. You can even see what your
name would look like in Viking runes!

Vikings: The North Atlantic Saga
www.mnh.si.edu/vikings/
This Smithsonian Web site features great videos
and text about Viking voyages and wonderful
audio commentary. The site starts off with
an amazing Flash-animated introduction.

Index

Index

About the Author

Aileen Weintraub is a freelance author and editor living in the scenic Hudson Valley in upstate New York. She has published over thirty-five books for children and young adults.